BASKETBALL

Strategy on the Hardwood

PREPARING FOR GAME DAY

BASEBALL & SOFTBALL: SUCCESS ON THE DIAMOND

BASKETBALL: STRATEGY ON THE HARDWOOD

CHEERLEADING: TECHNIQUES FOR PERFORMING

EXTREME SPORTS: POINTERS FOR PUSHING THE LIMITS

FOOTBALL: TOUGHNESS ON THE GRIDIRON

LACROSSE: FACING OFF ON THE FIELD

SOCCER: BREAKING AWAY ON THE PITCH

TRACK & FIELD: CONDITIONING FOR GREATNESS

VOLLEYBALL: APPROACHING THE NET

WRESTLING: CONTENDING ON THE MAT

PREPARING FOR GAME DAY

BASKETBALL
Strategy on the Hardwood

Peter Douglas

MASON CREST

Mason Crest
450 Parkway Drive, Suite D
Broomall, Pennsylvania 19008
(866) MCP-BOOK (toll free)

First printing
9 8 7 6 5 4 3 2 1

ISBN (hardback) 978-1-4222-3914-8
ISBN (series) 978-1-4222-3912-4
ISBN (ebook) 978-1-4222-7869-7

Cataloging-in-Publication Data on file with the Library of Congress

QR CODES AND LINKS TO THIRD-PARTY CONTENT

CONTENTS

CHAPTER 1   Game Day 7

CHAPTER 2   Think the Game 19

CHAPTER 3   Physical Preparation 29

CHAPTER 4   Taking Care of the Body:
Injuries and Nutrition 45

CHAPTER 5   Basketball: From Set Shots to Slam
Dunks and Small Ball 59

Series Glossary of Key Terms 72

Further Reading, Video Credits,
& Internet Resources 74

Index 77

KEY ICONS TO LOOK FOR:

Words to understand: These words with their easy-to-understand definitions will increase the reader's understanding of the text while building vocabulary skills.

Sidebars: This boxed material within the main text allows readers to build knowledge, gain insights, explore possibilities, and broaden their perspectives by weaving together additional information to provide realistic and holistic perspectives.

Educational Videos: Readers can view videos by scanning our QR codes, providing them with additional educational content to supplement the text. Examples include news coverage, moments in history, speeches, iconic sports moments and much more!

Text-dependent questions: These questions send the reader back to the text for more careful attention to the evidence presented there.

Research projects: Readers are pointed toward areas of further inquiry connected to each chapter. Suggestions are provided for projects that encourage deeper research and analysis.

Series glossary of key terms: This back-of-the book glossary contains terminology used throughout this series. Words found here increase the reader's ability to read and comprehend higher-level books and articles in this field.

WORDS TO UNDERSTAND:

cadence: a regular beat or rhythm

complement: to enhance by providing something additional

simulating: looking, feeling, or behaving like something

Chapter

GAME DAY

After an off-season of studying plays, training, and conditioning, or in season after practicing drill after drill, the day or night comes when it is time to put practice aside and play the game. In the chapters that follow, we will look

UCLA coaching legend John Wooden

at how to be physically and mentally prepared to play, but on that given day, important steps are necessary to ensure all the tough hours of preparation are not wasted. Game day preparation is a key component to a basketball player's success.

"Failing to prepare is preparing to fail."

— *John Wooden, UCLA Men's Basketball Coach 1948-1975*

Getting your "game face" on is a common sports expression, but it captures an important aspect of being ready to play. Players need to be in the right mind-set to perform at their best, blocking out distractions to focus on the task at hand. And while ultimately that task is to win the game, the best way to do that is to be a good teammate. Part of preparation means knowing your role on the team, knowing the game plan, and sticking to it. This unselfish play will help to make it easier for the other players on the team to do their jobs and thus make them better.

> "For a game day, I'll get a room service breakfast at like 9 a.m. I like omelets or sausage-and-egg biscuits or waffles or fruit. That's the biggest thing for me. I have to eat breakfast, and if I don't, my metabolism just isn't working and it's not good for me. I find if I miss break-fast, it's hard for me to keep weight."
>
> – Mike Muscala, NBA power forward

One of the big keys to being at your best at game time is paying attention to maintaining proper game day nutrition. Without the right kind of fuel, optimal performance will be hard to reach. A healthy, balanced diet is important for athletes like basketball players every day, but on game day, there are special nutritional needs that should be met to prepare the body for the massive energy burn to come. Experts recommend a high carbohydrate meal about two to three hours before game time for basketball players. Complex carbohydrates will provide a consistent supply of energy as they break down in your system throughout the game. Examples of good pregame meal choices include whole wheat pasta or peanut butter or submarine sandwiches.

> " If you nap every game day, all those hours add up, and it allows you to get through the season better. "
>
> — Steve Nash, two-time NBA MVP

If there is no time for a large meal, it is a good idea to have a snack about an hour before playing. Items like nuts and fruit make good snacks, with the fruit providing carbohydrates with natural sugar and nuts providing protein.

Celtics legend Bill Russell looks up at a shot going through the hoop

"One thing consistently I have always done, starting in high school, is I take a nap before the game. We had shootaround in high school, and I'd go back home and take an hour or two nap before the game. Now it's like three or four hours and just relax and have the energy for the night."

— LeBron James, Four-time NBA MVP

Eating the right thing at the right time is crucial, but it would be a missed opportunity to fuel a body that is not well rested. Getting the proper amount of sleep is essential to preparing the body to perform at an optimal level on game day. This certainly applies to sleeping well the night before a game day, but given the fact that most basketball games are played in the evenings, many players also work in a game day nap as well.

Players will sleep anywhere from one to three hours, waking up about four hours before game time. For college and professional players who travel extensively, the midday nap is often the most consistent rest they get in their routine. Experts stress the importance of proper rest as it is said to enhance reaction time and energy levels.

Properly fed and rested, most players at the college and professional levels arrive at the arena about three hours before tip-off. After changing out of street clothes, the next key element in game day preparation is stretching. Stretching has a number of benefits that prepare a player's body for all the running, jumping, and sudden changes in direction about to come. A consistent stretching routine will increase flexibility in muscles and tendons. Coaches recommend twenty to thirty minutes to maximize flexibility before games. Better flexibility means better range of motion, which translates to longer strides and longer reach.

Stretching also promotes better balance between muscle groups. Basketball stresses opposing muscle groups to different degrees (i.e., the quadriceps vs. the hamstrings), which can lead to an imbalance in the way muscles develop. The result of this imbalance is often pain in the joint they surround (i.e., the knee). Stretching before games helps to balance out all the major muscle groups.

> *"I didn't really understand the importance of stretching until I started playing college basketball. I had to make sure my body was prepared to perform at a high level. Stretching before you play helps performance and injury prevention. Stretching after you play helps with muscle fatigue."*
> — *Lamar Hull, NCAA DI point guard*

> Set a goal that stretches you, requires exceptional effort, but one that you can reach.
> — Pat Summitt, eight-time NCAA women's champion coach

Stretching is an effective way to help prevent injuries. Common ailments of the sport such as ligament tears and sprains or pulled muscles can be avoided by stretching them all properly before playing. Stretching is the best preventative measure against most common basketball injuries.

Players might not always be thinking about after the game before the game has even started, but in terms of their bodies and health, they should. Stretching before playing is a good way to help the body recover well after playing. It improves blood flow and circulation, which allows your body to get reparative oxygen to sore muscles more efficiently. The more you stretch before, the faster you feel better after the game.

After a solid twenty- to thirty-minute stretching routine, players then go through warm-ups. Different teams use different approaches to warm-ups. Some will concentrate on basketball drills. In addition to literally warming up the body and keeping muscles loose, pregame warm-up drills also reinforce the fundamentals of the plan for that game. Drills such as two-line layups, four-line passing, and four-corner layups are common warm-up staples.

> "When you're out there shooting (warm-ups), it's no good to shoot shots that don't have any meaning. You shoot the shots that you're going to get in the game."
>
> – George Hill,
> NBA point guard

Other teams will opt for calisthenics or other forms of dynamic exercise to warm up. These exercises incorporate basketball movements like jogging, backpedaling, and lateral shuffling. Dynamic warm-ups can also include tools such as a speed ladder or jump rope, which can help with footwork or with warming up both the upper and lower body. Some players, like Golden State's Stephen Curry, work on ball skills. Curry's pregame routine is so spectacular that fans fill the stands hours before tip-off to watch it.

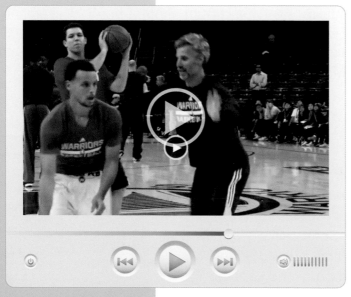

Check out Golden State superstar Steph Curry's warm-up routine.

Following warm-up drills and exercises, most teams engage in what is commonly known as the shootaround. Shootarounds involve players taking practice shot after practice shot from various spots around the court. Although it may look random to the uninitiated, players use the shootaround for a specific purpose. For some, it is about trying to find a shooting rhythm, the pace or **cadence** in a shot-taking routine that results in the majority of shots going in the basket. For others, it is about **simulating** the types of shots they are most likely to take in a game to build confidence in making each attempt. Yet others try to get to a particular number of made shots. Ideally, every element of the shootaround should represent a small part of the larger offense. Every

> "I think when you try to warm up, you try to go with the spot-up (jump shot) at the beginning just to get a rhythm going on."
>
> – José Calderón,
>   NBA point guard

Jose Calderon of the Toronto Raptors dribbles the ball during a game against the Detroit Pistons in Michigan.

Former Chicago Bulls superstar and NBA Hall of Famer Michael Jordan

drill, exercise, and shooting sequence should have a specific purpose.

After the shootaround ends and the court is being prepared for the game to come, players should use this time to prepare their minds. Players focus on plugging into the right mind-set, a positive way of approaching the game that best promotes a chance at a successful outcome. This can involve different things for different players. A proper pregame mental routine will allow players to focus on the game while blocking out external distractions. It should allow them to relax while concentrating on affirming in their minds the strength of their talents and the depth of their hard work. Some athletes like to listen to music immediately before the game, which for many is effective in allowing them to tune out and focus.

Another routine used by many players involves imagery and visualization. Typically, although not always, this is done with the eyes closed. Players breathe deeply and evenly and focus on seeing themselves perform successfully on the court. They focus on what it looks like when the ball leaves their hands and travels in the correct arc to fall through the basket. They not only imagine the way this looks, but they also think of the way the ball feels coming off their fingertips on the shot release, of the sound the ball makes as it rips through the net, of the cheering of the crowd.

Some players also believe in the power of affirmations, positive sayings recited aloud that reinforce the hard work and hours of practice that lead up to games. These sayings are not results based but rather designed to instill confidence, emphasize that what is important is to do your best for yourself and your teammates, and remind you to have fun playing.

"I'm not out there sweating for three hours every day just to find out what it feels like to sweat."

— Michael Jordan, five-time NBA MVP

There are many professional and college teams that use sports psychologists to help get their teams mentally ready to play a game. These are mental health professionals that design mental pregame routines for individual players that help them be mentally tough in their approach to games. This is something that takes work and practice but when done successfully can have a positive impact on a player's ability to focus on playing his or her best game and not letting mistakes or opponents get in their heads.

Players call it "getting in the zone," which means achieving a positive mental state of preparedness to play. When you are in the zone, it is difficult for opposing players to get you off your game. A well-constructed mental routine should last about twenty minutes and **complement** all the hard physical work that went into preparing for the game. It does little good for players to be in top physical condition if mentally they do not have confidence and approach each game prepared to succeed.

> *"The extra pass and the extra effort on defense always get the job done."*
>
> — *Kareem Abdul-Jabbar, six-time NBA MVP*

> *"I used a lot of visualization in terms of who I would be guarding and who would be guarding me. I'd imagine those individuals in front of me. I'd imagine going around them."*
>
> — *Isiah Thomas, two-time NBA champion*

TEXT-DEPENDENT QUESTIONS:

1. Name one of the biggest keys to being at your best at game time.

2. What activity promotes better balance between muscle groups?

3. What kind of warm-ups can include tools such as a speed ladder or jump rope?

RESEARCH PROJECT:

Take some time, and put together a pregame routine for yourself. Be detailed in each element, outlining specific numbers of repetitions for drills, shots taken, and so on. Outline meals, rest, and all the necessary components that you feel could help best prepare you before a big game.

WORDS TO UNDERSTAND:

enhancement: increase or improvement in value, quality, desirability, or attractiveness

optimal: most desirable or satisfactory

spectrum: a complete range

Chapter 2

THINK THE GAME

Confidence is a big part of a good performer's approach to playing any sport. Confidence, however, does not only come from being physically prepared. Being ready to play mentally is no less important an ingredient to playing at an **optimal** level. Practicing that jump shot and hours of ball handling drills are necessary, but being focused, mentally sharp, in the right state of mind—and knowing the game plan—are the keys to a good performance.

> The key is not the "will to win."... Everybody has that. It is the will to prepare to win that is important.
>
> – Bob Knight, Indiana University head coach, 1971–2000

Basketball strategy is an important mental component of the game.

Players huddle during a time-out, which coaches use strategically to change momentum in games.

THE Xs AND Os

Coaches at all levels of basketball spend time working on the strategy of the game and on preparing players to execute that strategy. Sound strategies are based not only on your team's strengths but also on your expectations of the opponent. For those strategies to work, players must be mentally prepared to execute them. That means time in the classroom watching video of opponents and themselves. And it means time studying the playbook to know what to do in given situations. Some examples of commonly used plays include the following:

OFFENSE

- **Pick and roll**—A pick (or screen) occurs when a player stands stationary in a position that allows his teammate who has the ball to use him as an obstacle between the teammate and a pursuing defender. The player then "rolls" off when the defender goes around and accepts a pass from his teammate.

- **Fast break**—This play is the immediate transition from defense to offense and is usually initiated off of a defensive rebound. The idea is to get behind the defense before they can get set, so they have to chase the play. This is done using an outlet pass from the rebounder to a teammate breaking quickly toward the other basket.

- **Give-and-go**—A player being guarded by a defender passes the ball to an open teammate and immediately cuts toward the basket. The teammate returns the pass to the player, who usually has an open lane to the basket. This play often works because the defender guarding the first player will follow the ball and switch to the second player.

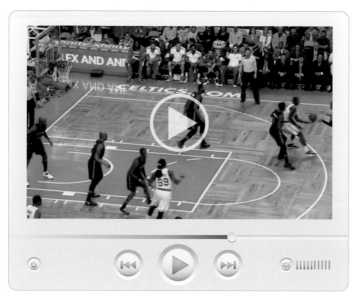

Check out this video of an Xs and Os demo of an NBA play.

DEFENSE

- **Full-court press**—Defensive players initiate a man-to-man defense in the opponent's backcourt when they are attempting to inbound the ball. This is intended to force a turnover or a ten-second violation.

- **Late game fouls**—When an opponent leading late in a game is in the bonus, a good strategy is to commit fouls. Fouling stops the clock and forces the opponent to make free throws. This strategy is dependent on a few things: fouling players that are not good free throw shooters (if the team makes its free throws, they will not be caught); making shots on your own possessions to close the gap; and not being called for intentional fouls. Fouls must be in the natural flow of the game. If the referee calls an intentional foul, the opponent retains possession of the ball after shooting free throws.

- **Time-out**—Coaches try to use time-outs strategically, usually calling them when the opponent is having the better of the play, so they can regroup with their players and discuss tactics to regain control of the game.

realistically as possible. "You can't imagine every possible scenario," said Detling, "so do the obvious ones and then maybe a couple of unexpected ones."

Imagery requires practice to get the most from it, and Detling says people with active imaginations are better at it. But she stressed, "When you are at the actual performance, you've got to be able to pull it from your head."

> *This is like visualizing plus. It allows me not only to see the ball go in the basket but to feel my mechanics and most importantly as a shooter, to feel your rhythm.*
>
> *Steve Nash, eight-time NBA all-star.*

RELAXED ATTENTION

Another common practice among athletes is relaxed attention. Playing while keeping tension, thoughts, and emotions under control is the key to this technique. One common example is the pre-shot ritual some basketball players go through at the free throw line, usually bouncing the ball a certain number of times or spinning it a certain way. They are practicing relaxed attention. Mistakes can be avoided if players can control anger and anxiety. Confidence and a calm attitude can make the difference in a closely contested game. Being mentally prepared is the necessary complement to being physically ready for teams that aspire to win.

MEDITATION

Panic, anxiety, and worry are the signs of an unprepared mind. An athlete that is properly prepared will be calm, determined, and focused. Many athletes use meditation as part of that preparation. Meditation is the practice of quieting the mind, bypassing thinking to achieve a more relaxed state. If players master this technique, they can employ it as needed during pressure situations to mentally remove and calm themselves during high-stress situations. Some of the benefits of meditation are increased confidence, decreased heart rate, reduced anxiety, and better blood flow.

SIDEBAR

Unique Superstitions of Basketball Stars

1. Stroke My Face
New York Knicks head coach Jeff Hornacek played fourteen years in the NBA, where he was an all-star shooting guard. He took thousands of free throws in his career, and before every one, he stroked the side of his face several times. This unusual pre-shot routine was his secret way of him waving and saying "hi" to his three kids.

2. Streets, Socks, and Gum
Hall of Fame center Shaquille O'Neal drove on the same streets to the arena every time he had a game. Once he got to the arena, when he got dressed he always wore two pairs of socks for every game. O'Neal also chewed exactly four pieces of gum before every game, and then he had to stick the wad underneath his seat on the bench.

3. Shake My Hand
Four-time NBA MVP LeBron James is famous for his chalk-tossing routine, but his most personalized superstition is the secret handshakes he shares with every one of his teammates. James has a different handshake for each teammate, and without fail, he does that handshake pregame with each one.

4. Hit the Showers
Four-time all-star and NBA champion Rajon Rondo may be the cleanest person in the NBA. He likes to shower before each game, which is not that strange. The thing about Rondo, however, is he has to shower five separate times.

5. Pop, Straws, and More Pop
Two-time all-star and NBA champion forward Caron Butler did not have a particularly healthy superstition early in his career. Prior to every game, Butler would drink half a two-liter bottle of Mountain Dew. He also took exactly twelve drinking straws from McDonald's or Burger King restaurants and would chew on them when sitting on the bench during the game. Then at halftime, he would drink the other half of that bottle of pop. His team eventually banned both practices.

Michael Jordan's game day superstition involved wearing his old college shorts under his NBA uniform shorts for every game.

SUPERSTITION

On the negative end of the mental **spectrum** is superstition. Superstition is the belief that there is a causal relationship between two unrelated things, like winning a game because you are wearing a certain pair of socks. Although superstitious acts may help athletes gain confidence if the superstition has been followed, it can also cause anxiety if for some reason it has not. One famous example is Hall of Fame guard Michael Jordan of the Chicago Bulls' belief that his old practice shorts from college were lucky. He always wore them under his Bulls shorts during NBA games. Point guard Jason Terry would sleep in the game-worn shorts of the opponents he was playing the next day. LeBron James famously throws chalk in the air and claps his hands together right before games. In 2012, each member of the Boston Celtics ate a peanut butter and jelly sandwich an hour before games. On every game day of his entire career, Ray Allen slept from 11 a.m. to 1 p.m., ate chicken and rice at 2:30 p.m., and shaved his head right before going out for warm-ups at 3:30 p.m. As long as they help the athlete to be more confident, it doesn't matter whether these superstitions have anything to do with good luck or not.

TEXT-DEPENDENT QUESTIONS:

1. What is a "pick and roll"?

2. The practice of visualization has been around since what decade?

3. What is the practice of quieting the mind and bypassing thinking to achieve a more relaxed state?

RESEARCH PROJECT:

The next few times you prepare for a game, or other activity, alternate using imagery versus not using it. Note the differences in your performance. Does using imagery make a difference?

WORDS TO UNDERSTAND:

aerobically: involving, utilizing, or increasing oxygen consumption for metabolic processes in the body

lateral: extending from side to side

supple: soft and able to bend or fold easily

Chapter 3

PHYSICAL PREPARATION

Basketball is not a contact sport. Person-to-person contact is considered to be a foul and is illegal. However, with all of the starting, stopping, and sudden **lateral** movement, non-contact injuries like ligament sprains and muscle strains are common. One way to help avoid these kinds of injuries is to warm up before playing.

Not only do warm-ups help to prepare the body for the rigors of a game, but they are also a good rehearsal of basketball skills. Warm-ups usually start off with light work such as stretches, bounce passes, and jump shots. Crisp chest passes follow as the pace picks up and players work on loosening their arm and upper

The Milwaukee Bucks and Philadelphia 76ers participate in pregame warm-ups prior to an NBA game in Milwaukee.

body muscles. Rebounding drills are typically next, as players switch off making running layups and grabbing rebounds to break a light sweat. And while warming up is the primary purpose of these activities to make sure muscles and tendons are ready for game conditions, basketball skills also get a last-minute polish.

The moderate exercise also prepares a player's body for the considerable demands on the respiratory system. At the collegiate and professional levels, many of the games feature TV time-outs, where the action stops for several minutes as the TV network broadcasting the games airs commercials. At the high school level, however, stoppages are very brief, and the cardiovascular requirements demanded by the up-and-down action are considerable.

WARM-UP AND PRECONDITIONING

It does not take a lot of time for a warm-up to be effective. Muscles, ligaments, and tendons benefit from just fifteen minutes of stretching by having increased flexibility. Loosening up should take place starting from the neck and working down to the legs. **Supple** muscles and joints are less likely to be strained, pulled, or torn. Even light aerobic exercise like warm-up drills help the body by increasing its capacity to intake oxygen, which is usually noticeable in less than one minute.

Pregame warm-ups on the court are usually limited to stretching and light drills as more intensive calisthenics like jumping jacks or even light jogging are not advisable on the hard court surface. The body, especially the knees and lower back, will take enough of a pounding during the game. If a player

Stretching is an important part of a basketball player's pregame routine.

SIDEBAR

Conditioning Tips

- Before any exercise session, always remember first to do a light warm-up and to stretch.

- Begin your conditioning program by exercising lightly, from thirty minutes to an hour, depending on your fitness level. Slowly increase the time each day. It will take from six to eight weeks to reach top condition.

- Do not exercise or practice basketball for more than ninety minutes each session. The key to conditioning is physical intensity and concentration, not longer workouts.

- Select exercises for flexibility and strength, and add relaxation techniques that were discussed in Chapter 2.

- Exercise to the full capacity of your body's limits, but never endanger your health or safety by going beyond them.

wants to do more intensive exercise, that happens in the locker room before coming out to the court for warm-ups.

Cooling down following a game is also an important element of player health. Two to five minutes of cool-down time is typical and helps to regulate breathing and bring the heart rate to normal levels. The muscles in the body are full of blood after a strenuous game as the heart has worked hard to supply them with oxygen. If that blood stays in the muscles, the result can be soreness and stiffness. Cooling down by walking or stretching will remedy this issue. One of the worst things to do is to sit down immediately after as this can cause dizziness or fainting.

Year-round conditioning is now the norm in professional sports. In decades past, many athletes used training camp to get back in top shape. Today's

Scan here to see NBA all-star Chris Paul's workout video.

athletes, however, work throughout the off-season and come to training camp in top condition. This kind of dedication is important to succeed at any level. Being in top condition is a great way to stave off injury. Some good off-season workouts for basketball players include running, swimming, and cycling. Players should plan on at least thirty minutes of working out three times a week. Weight training is not encouraged in young athletes as this kind of activity has been shown to damage underdeveloped cartilage.

EXERCISING TO BE FLEXIBLE

Upper body warm-up exercises concentrate on the neck, arms, shoulders, waist, and back. Here are few good ones:

- Stretch the neck by grabbing the back of the head with the right hand and pulling the head to the right. Repeat with the left hand.

- Stretch the arms upward and backward.

- Reach the arms toward the sky one at a time.

- Rotate the arms forward in circles on either side, moving one up as the other descends.

- Hold each elbow behind the head in a pulling motion.

- Raise the arms to shoulder level, pulling them back and holding the position.

- Raise the shoulders while keeping the arms next to the body, and then move the shoulders backward in slow circles and then forward.

- For the waist, hold the arms out to the side and swing them as you twist your body back and forth to the right and left.

- For the back, lie on your front with your legs crossed at the ankles and your arms straight out in front. Raise your upper body off the floor five times, holding each time for one second, and then slowly lower back to the floor.

Flexibility exercises for the lower body are extremely important in basketball. These are usually done either sitting or lying down. Here is a collection of stretches for the muscles from the lower back to the toes:

- Pointed toes: Walk on your heels with your feet flexed—toes pointed—to keep your shin muscles tightened. Walk about ten yards four times.

- Side lunge: To stretch your hamstrings and thighs, stand in a straddle position facing forward. Slowly lean to your right while keeping your back straight and your feet at forty-five degrees. Keep your left knee from moving past your right foot, and point the toes of your left foot upwards. Hold this position for fifteen seconds, then switch legs, and repeat twice.

Flexibility exercises for the lower body are extremely important in basketball.

- Lying crossover: Lie on your back with both legs extended to one side. Lift your right leg and cross it over your body, resting it close to your left hand, keeping your shoulders flat on the ground. Hold for ten to fifteen seconds, and then switch sides. This stretches the buttocks, lower spine, and oblique muscles.

- Groin stretch: Sit down with your knees bent, facing outward, and the bottom of your feet touching one another. Slowly stretch your legs, pressing your knees as close to the ground as you can, then hold for fifteen seconds. Repeat.

TRAINING

Along with conditioning the body **aerobically** and preparing it by stretching, basketball players also need to train the body in certain other aspects as well. Examples of this include weight training, resistance training, plyometrics, and cardio training.

WEIGHT TRAINING

Weight training is designed to build the strength needed in both the upper and lower body. Upper body strength helps when fighting for rebounds and loose balls. Lower body strength provides power when jumping and running up the court.

For basketball, players need to work constantly to improve not only strength but also their quickness and vertical jump if they want to stay competitive. Weight training is a tool for doing just that.

Here is a sample weight lifting routine from Stack.com that is ideal for basketball players during the off-season, when the hardest and most intense lifting should be done. The amount of weight to be used depends on the strength and ability level of the player. Perform each exercise as explosively as possible. Practice good form, and always lift with a spotter.

MONDAY
Chest/Triceps

Bench Press—3X10

Incline Dumbbell Press—2X10

Tricep Dips—2X12

Tricep Pushdowns—2X10

Burpee Push-Ups—2X10

TUESDAY
Legs

Dumbell Squats—3X12, 10, 8

Dumbbell Lunge—3X2

Bounding—3X10

Depth Jumps—2X12

Jump Rope—5X30-45 seconds

WEDNESDAY

Rest

This is an important component.
The body needs time to recover.

THURSDAY
Back/Shoulders/Biceps

Pull-Ups—3X8

Dumbbell Shoulder Press —3X12

Cable Seated Row—3X10

Dumbbell Front Shoulder Raise—2X10

Dumbbell Lateral Shoulder Raise—2X10

Bicep Curls—3X10

Hammer Curls—3X10

FRIDAY
Legs

Knee Tucks—2X20

Lunge Jumps—3X12

Box Jumps—3X8

The bench press is a good exercise to include in a basketball player's weekly weight training routine.

RESISTANCE TRAINING

In resistance training, the results are similar to those of weight training, but rather than lifting heavy objects, the athlete moves against something that is resisting in the opposite direction, which can be resistance bands, another person, or his or her own body weight. Here are some examples of resistance exercises that are beneficial for basketball players.

Plank—2x60 seconds: The athlete assumes a position on the floor resting only on the forearms and toes, with the torso parallel to the floor. Variations to this include holding one leg off the floor and alternating after thirty seconds or bringing the knees to the chest, alternating legs after thirty seconds. This exercise helps to build core strength.

Crunches—2x30: The athlete lies flat on his or her back with knees bent and feet flat on the floor hip-width apart, places the fingertips against the

head around the ears. While pressing the small of the back into the floor, the player rolls the shoulders forward and up off the floor about four inches. He or she holds that position for one second each time before lowering back down and repeating. This is another excellent exercise to build core strength.

Band-Resisted Backboard Touches—3x10: Wearing resistance bands over each shoulder that wrap under the opposite foot, the player crouches in an athletic position and then jumps with arms extended, reaching for the backboard. This is a lower body exercise.

Speed Dribble with Harness—3x15 seconds: The player wears a harness around the torso that is attached at the back to resistance bands. With a coach or training partner holding on to the bands, the player attempts to dribble a ball forward while the person holding the bands works to hold him or her back.

Band-Resisted Layups—3x8: The player wears a harness attached to resistance bands for this drill. He or she stands under the basket, going from one side of the rim to the other doing layups, while the person holding the bands attempts to prevent the player from jumping.

Crunches are a popular resistance training exercise.

Jumping rope helps strengthen the legs while improving cardiovascular fitness and footwork.

PLYOMETRICS

Commonly referred to as "plyos" in sports lingo, plyometric exercises are a very important part of basketball training. Plyometrics are exercise drills that involve movements like jumping, hopping, sprinting, or quick movements for the upper body. These actions train the body to jump higher, faster, and react quicker. They are designed to increase balance, coordination, quickness, flexibility, conditioning, and overall strength and power. Through muscle memory, the nervous system will allow the body to automatically react on the court during a game. Here are some examples of plyo exercises:

- The Skier is an exercise that works to quicken foot speed and improve overall explosiveness and physical condition. It can be performed on the court or any stable surface. Stand with the knees bent in a downhill skiing tuck position, and then jump from one side to the other, with feet barely touching the ground as though they are landing on a hot surface. Start with two thirty-second sets with thirty seconds in between. As stamina and skills increase, so should the duration of each drill.

- Plank Ski Jumps aim to improve core strength and overall condition. Start with two sets, lasting for about thirty seconds each, with a rest

period in between lasting the same amount of time. Assume the push-up or plank position. Without moving the hands and keeping the feet together, jump them up and to the outside of the right hand. Immediately jump them back to the start position, then immediately to the outside of the left hand, and then back to the start. Repeat with no pauses, increasing the length of each set as endurance increases.

Although plyometrics is a vital part of training, it should never be overdone. In fact, basketball is a plyometrics workout in itself, so adding plyometric exercises in season can be more harmful than helpful.

CARDIOVASCULAR TRAINING

The final piece to the puzzle in keeping fit for basketball is cardiovascular training, or cardio for short. If you have the skills to outplay your opponent, they will do no good if you are unable to keep up with them throughout the game. Being in top physical condition once basketball season rolls around is essential, and endurance is a huge part of this.

Swimming is a great off-season exercise to help basketball players stay in shape.

First, a good aerobic workout routine is key. You should establish a routine that consists of thirty to forty-five minutes of activity three to four days a week. The most common cardio activity for athletes is running, but there are many options.

- Stationary bike: 30–45 minutes
- Running: 30 minutes
- Elliptical machine: 30 minutes
- Calisthenics: 30 minutes
- Swimming: 30 minutes

As this list of suggested exercises demonstrates, it is important to maintain a mix of different workouts. There are a number of reasons for this.

For example, while running is very effective, it can become stressful on the body if it is done for long periods. You are at a higher risk of injury if you only take part in one activity as opposed to a variety, and by being creative with your workouts, they may not become boring and monotonous.

Second, interval training that includes anaerobic activity (short-duration, high-intensity exercise) is a must. The goal of interval training is to condition your body to become accustomed to the high-intensity running, and the brief time-outs that often follow, that are very specific to basketball (e.g., while another player is taking a foul shot, and you are watching, trying to catch your breath). These anaerobic sessions should range from a 1:1 to a 1:3 work/rest ratio to best imitate activity during an actual game (i.e., if you exercise for ten minutes, you should rest for ten to thirty minutes.)

Stretching thoroughly before starting any activity, especially interval training, is vital. In addition to your general warm-up and stretching, you should also include a sprint-specific warm-up to ready your muscles for anaerobic workouts.

Basketball-specific metabolic training is the third and final stage of a well-rounded cardio workout. This preparation includes metabolic conditioning as well as basketball drills. Here is a detailed example:

- Start on the baseline, and sprint to the free throw line and back.

- Immediately sprint to the opposite baseline and back.

- Immediately sprint to half-court, and backpedal back.

- Rest twenty-five seconds.

- Laterally slide to the free throw line (with a left arm lead), and slide back.

- Sprint to half-court, and backpedal back.

- Laterally slide to the free-throw line (with a right arm lead), and slide back.

- Rest twenty-five seconds.

- Repeat this drill for a total of six repetitions, changing the commands each time.

Players should rest for two minutes between repetitions. This rest period is a good time to practice free throws, with a high heart rate and heavy breathing simulating game conditions. Depending on your current conditioning level, you can adjust the amount of repetitions, but always aim for the maximum amount you feel you can do without pushing yourself too hard, which can lead to injury.

It is best that any off-season program is practiced under the supervision of a coach or a personal trainer. If you perform these exercises without the right techniques, you can do your body more harm than good. The first few times that you lift in the weight room, you should have one-on-one instruction on how to handle the weights, and you should never lift alone.

TEXT-DEPENDENT QUESTIONS:

1. Name three conditioning tips.

2. What are plyometrics?

3. A good aerobic workout routine consists of how many minutes of cardio activity three to four days a week?

RESEARCH PROJECT:

Run for forty-five minutes on the treadmill, and make note of how far you are able to go. Reduce your running time to forty minutes, and make note of the distance you can run in that time. Track how long it takes before you can run the same distance in forty minutes that you were able to initially in forty-five minutes. Then reduce running time to thirty-five minutes, and do the same thing. Compare how long it took to match the forty-five-minute time in forty minutes to how long it took to match the forty-minute time in thirty-five minutes.

WORDS TO UNDERSTAND:

conjunction: a situation in which two or more things happen at the same time or in the same place

refraining: stopping yourself from doing something that you want to do

supplements: something that completes or adds to

Chapter 4

TAKING CARE OF THE BODY: INJURIES AND NUTRITION

A survey by the U.S. Consumer Product Safety Commission found that for kids aged five to fourteen, more than 170,000 basketball-related injuries occur annually, behind only football and cycling among all recreational activities.

As basketball is a non-contact sport, there is very little in the way of protective equipment. Mouth guards will protect the mouth and teeth. Safety glasses should be worn in place of regular glasses. Knee and elbow pads, while they aren't regularly used, offer good protection from bruises and scrapes that occur on the court, and ankle supports can be worn to reduce the chance of ankle sprains. But the best equipment to prevent injuries is a good pair of basketball shoes. They should have solid support, fit snugly, and have good traction to reduce slipping.

The condition of the court itself also plays a role in player safety. The backboard and all supporting bars must be adequately secured and padded, and the walls behind the baskets should be padded as well and never too close to the baskets. The officials' table should not be near the boundary lines, bleachers, or other

More than 170,000 basketball-related injuries occur every year.

structures. The floor must be clean, without debris, and definitely not slippery. If a game is played outside, it is very important to check for natural hazards, such as holes and rocks.

TYPES OF INJURIES

During a game, players should be alert to the danger of collisions, keeping an eye on other players' movements. Another way of reducing injuries is to play fair, **refraining** from tripping, pushing, holding, elbowing, blocking, or charging into opponents. Even if players do their best to avoid these fouls, however, various types of injuries due to collisions or falls still occur.

ACUTE OR ACUTE TRAUMATIC INJURIES

This can be caused by a bad fall or any hard hit during a game, such as a collision with another player. Acute injuries include contusions, abrasions, lacerations, sprains, strains, and fractures. "Contusion" is the medical name for a bruise, which may be bad enough to cause swelling and bleeding in the muscles or other tissues. An abrasion is a scrape, and a laceration is a cut that is usually deep enough to require stitches. A sprain is a stretch or tear of a ligament, which is the tissue that supports joints by connecting bones and cartilage. If a stretch or tear occurs in a muscle or tendon (the tissue that connects muscles to bones), this is a strain. A fracture involves a crack, break, or shattering of a bone.

OVERUSE OR CHRONIC INJURIES

This kind of injury is caused by repeating the same action many times, as when a center rebounds the ball over and over until experiencing an ache in the ankles or knees. This is not as serious as an acute injury, but any chronic problem may become worse during the season, so players should seek medical advice and treatment.

COMMON INJURIES

The lower body is where injuries occur most often, but the upper body, including the head, can also sustain injuries, particularly in a hard fall. For many injuries, a combination of rest, ice, compression and elevation (R.I.C.E. treatment) can reduce their severity and aid in healing.

ANKLE AND FOOT INJURIES

The feet and ankles do the bulk of the work in basketball and therefore are the areas most often injured. The most common plays, such as quickly cutting around a defensive player or leaping high for a rebound, may result in an uncertain landing, subjecting ankles and feet to continuous stress. Young players put additional wear and tear on these parts when they play on outdoor, concrete courts. The strenuous action on any court can result in ankle sprains, heel bruises, and fractures. A sprain that severely stretches the ligaments of the outside ankle is fairly common in basketball because players make rapid changes in direction.

Foot and ankle injuries are among the most common that occur in basketball.

To avoid heel bruises, players should learn the proper technique for landing following a jump. Players can get painful bruises if they land on the base of their heels instead of their toes. Poorly fitting shoes may also bruise the heels where the Achilles tendon attaches the back of the heel to the muscles of the calf of the leg. Achilles tendonitis, in which the tendon becomes inflamed, is a common injury. The R.I.C.E. treatment is effective here.

Foot fractures can occur when another competitor lands on a player's foot, especially during rebounds. A bone can also develop tiny cracks from overuse, such as the running and leaping required by the game, and this is called a stress fracture. Any fracture may hurt and cause a limp.

CARTILAGE INJURIES

Knees and ankles are also susceptible to cartilage injuries. When the joint is twisted or stretched too far, the cartilage breaks off from the bone, causing swelling and pain. The joint will develop stiffness and popping sensations, and it might be difficult to extend or rotate the joint. Players who are still growing are more likely to suffer this injury; about one-third of these injuries will heal with rest, although it may also be necessary to wear a cast for several weeks. Usually, surgery is required in older teens and adults.

Falling on the court can cause a dislocated kneecap. This means the movable bone at the front of the knee (also called the patella) is pushed sideways, causing swelling and severe pain. A bulge can develop on the side of the knee, and walking may be affected.

Tendinitis is an inflammation of a tendon, which occurs in the knee and Achilles tendon in basketball players. This is an overuse injury caused by running and jumping, which stretches the tendon. The swelling can make bending the knee, trying to lift and extend the leg, or even simple walking very painful. Again, R.I.C.E. is the best treatment.

LEG

Leg injuries range from bruises to hamstring pulls; infrequent fractures are generally caused by falls. A leg contusion, or bruise, is a common injury,

Watch NBA guard Ricky Rubio as he recovers from injury.

especially in the quadriceps. The soreness can be reduced by ice packs, and the bruise will soon go away. Deeper bruises, however, rupture blood vessels in the area, and this blood can collect and cause serious problems if the muscle continues to be exercised. The most important part of the R.I.C.E. treatment for this injury is to elevate the leg to reduce blood pooling or collecting in one place.

Hamstring pulls (strains or tears) involve the large muscles at the back of the thigh and are usually caused by running and jumping. The muscle fibers are strained when a player runs fast and then suddenly changes the motion of the thigh from being pulled forward by the quadriceps to being pulled backward by the hamstrings. This injury will require about a four-week rest from playing.

HANDS, WRISTS, AND FINGERS

These areas are injured in a number of ways: receiving passes, shooting, rebounding, and breaking falls. Wrists are commonly sprained when the hand is bent too far forward or backward. The thumb and other fingers can be sprained, dislocated, jammed, or fractured when catching the ball or fallling. Players can also develop stress fractures in all of these bones. If the pain does not go away within twenty-four hours, athletes should consult a doctor. X-rays are needed, and treatment includes ice and, in the case of fractures, a splint.

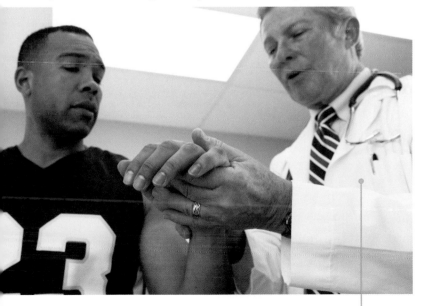

Hand and wrist injuries include jamming fingers on the ball and wrist fractures from falls.

SHOULDERS

Shoulders can be injured by overuse, which causes strain, inflammation, or tendinitis. More severe are the two main injuries caused by falls and collisions: a shoulder separation or a dislocation.

As soon as possible after an injury, such as a knee or ankle sprain, you can relieve pain and swelling and promote healing and flexibility with the R.I.C.E. treatment.

- Rest. Rest and protect the injured or sore area. Stop, change, or take a break from any activity that may be causing your pain or soreness.

- Ice. Cold will reduce pain and swelling. Apply an ice or cold pack right away to prevent or minimize swelling. Apply the ice or cold pack for ten to twenty minutes, three or more times a day. After forty-eight to seventy-two hours, if the swelling is gone, apply heat to the area that hurts. Do not apply ice or heat directly to the skin. Place a towel over the cold or heat pack before applying it.

- Compression. Compression, or wrapping the injured or sore area with an elastic bandage (such as an Ace wrap), will help decrease swelling. Don't wrap it too tightly, because this can cause more swelling below the affected area. Loosen the bandage if it gets too tight. Signs that the bandage is too tight include numbness, tingling, increased pain, coolness, or swelling in the area below the bandage. Talk to your doctor if you think you need to use a wrap for longer than forty-eight to seventy-two hours; a more serious problem may be present.

- Elevation. Elevate the injured or sore area on pillows while applying ice and anytime you are sitting or lying down. Try to keep the area at or above the level of your heart to help minimize swelling.

The separation of a shoulder involves a ligament tear that causes the collarbone to move upward. Rest normally corrects this in **conjunction** with strengthening exercises.

A dislocated shoulder occurs when the head of the humerus (upper arm bone) pops out of its socket. This requires immediate treatment. Torn cartilage or loose ligaments generally cause the dislocation. X-rays will be taken, and a shoulder sling should be worn for about three weeks. The most serious dislocations require surgery.

NECK

The most frequent neck injury in basketball is a "stinger" injury, which occurs when the nerves of the neck are overstretched, causing stinging pain and a temporary numbness. Pinched nerves, which can be caused by a quick sideways twist of the neck, produce a burning pain in both the neck and often down the arm. The standard treatment is once again the R.I.C.E. program. Minor neck injuries, including bruises and sprains, may require that the player wear a neck collar or brace. Much more dangerous is a fracture to the spine. This injury is very rare, but a player lying still on the court should not be moved until qualified emergency personnel arrive; movement could cause paralysis or death. X-rays will reveal the extent of the injury.

HEAD

Severe falls during play may also result in a concussion. This injury is normally mild, causing a headache, poor balance, a lack of alertness,

Although less common in basketball than in contact sports, concussions are taken seriously at every level.

memory loss, and sometimes unconsciousness. Increased awareness about long-term effects of concussions has led to more caution in allowing players to return from this injury. Any head injury will require a player to wait for at least a week or even a month after the symptoms disappear before returning to competition.

NUTRITION

For basketball players, nutrition is equally as important as conditioning and training. Athletes must be careful to eat a proper blend of nutrients to make sure their bodies and minds perform as well as they possibly can. More than just eating healthy foods, athletes also need to know when to eat, how much to eat, and whether to take dietary supplements.

Of course, when you choose a new diet or supplements, you should consult with a nutritionist, doctor, or other expert. Don't make up your own nutrition program!

WHAT TO EAT

Typically, an athlete has to eat considerably more than other people do, but they also have to pay careful attention to what they eat as well. The United States Food and Drug Administration (FDA) suggests that the average American should eat about 2,000 calories a day; for a male high school or college-level basketball player, a 3,000- to 4,000-calorie diet is more common. There are three main food groups to consider when choosing a diet: carbohydrates, protein, and fats.

CARBOHYDRATES

Starch-rich foods are high in carbohydrates, which is what the body breaks down to get energy. Starchy foods include breads and other grain-based food like cereal, pasta, and rice and vegetables such as potatoes. Roughly half an athlete's calories should come from carbohydrates, but they should beware of heavily processed carbohydrates such as sugary foods and white bread made with bleached flour. These foods are quickly broken down into sugars, which the body processes into fats if it does not immediately burn them off. The best carbohydrate choices for an athlete are pasta and whole-grain foods as well as starchy vegetables, which have vitamins as well as carbohydrates. A balanced diet avoids the "empty calories" supplied by white bread and sugars.

The best carbohydrate choices for an athlete are pasta and whole-grain foods as well as starchy vegetables.

PROTEIN

The cells that make up our bodies need proteins to help them perform certain functions. Each protein is a long, folded, chain-like molecule made up of "links" called amino acids. Our bodies can break down proteins into their base amino acids and use them to build new proteins that make up our muscles and bones. For this reason, it is important to eat enough protein to give the body the building blocks it needs to become stronger, especially during exercise. The best sources of proteins are meats and dairy products, such as milk or cheese, as well as eggs and certain vegetables (like soy

The best sources of proteins are meats and dairy products, such as milk or cheese, as well as eggs and beans.

or beans). To know how much protein to eat, a good rule of thumb is the number of grams should be equal to about one-third of your body weight in pounds. For example, a two hundred-pound person should have roughly seventy grams of protein per day.

FATS

Fat has a bad reputation as being unhealthy, but it is an important ingredient needed to make our bodies function correctly. Without fats, we could not absorb certain vitamins efficiently. Our skin and hair also need some amount of fat to grow correctly. However, fats should still be eaten in moderation— no more than seventy grams, or roughly 25 percent of total calories, per day. The best sources of fat are olive, canola, and peanut oils, fish, and nuts. Many foods contain saturated or trans fats, which lead to the formation of cholesterol and can force your heart to work harder.

DIETARY SUPPLEMENTS

Pills or drinks that contain nutrients or chemicals can help improve player performance during games. These dietary **supplements** do not include illegal performance-enhancing drugs. Instead, they contain vitamins, minerals, or chemicals that help the body use those vitamins more

Athletes should get no more than about 25 percent of their total calories per day from good fats like olive oil and nuts.

Multivitamins contain a balanced mixture of vitamins and nutrients.

efficiently. When properly used, supplements can improve overall health and performance, but athletes should always consult a doctor or nutritionist before taking them. Some examples of common supplements include vitamin tablets and protein shakes or powder.

VITAMIN TABLETS

Our diets are not as balanced as they should be, so we do not always get the vitamins and nutrients we need. Sometimes, it's because the foods available to us have been processed in such a way that they lose their nutrients. Also, exhausted soil in farms and orchards means that fruits and vegetables are often not as nutrient-rich as they should be. In many cases, we can get vitamins we need from vitamin supplements. These supplements, usually taken as pills, contain a balanced mixture of vitamins and nutrients known as multivitamins. Sometimes they contain a single vitamin or mineral that our diets are lacking. Be careful when taking vitamin supplements, however, because it is possible to overdose. Always talk to your doctor before beginning supplements of any kind.

PROTEIN SUPPLEMENTS

Eating protein immediately after a workout is recommended to refuel your body. The problem is that not many people feel up to preparing a meal right after exercising, so protein shakes are often a convenient and healthy choice. Many shakes contain blends of protein, carbohydrates, and fats, and some include vitamins to help balance your diet. Furthermore, having protein immediately after a workout can help repair the damage sustained by your muscles during exercise. You should always remember that although protein shakes are useful for supplementing your diet, they should never be used to replace meals in significant quantities. Your body still needs plenty of nutrients that it can get only from a balanced diet. No matter how fortified a protein shake may be, it cannot adequately replace a real meal. A nutritionist can tell you how to fit protein or supplement shakes into your diet safely and effectively.

Protein shakes are useful for supplementing diets, but they should never be used to replace meals in significant quantities.

TEXT-DEPENDENT QUESTIONS:

1. Name three acute injuries.

2. The FDA suggests that the average American should eat about 2,000 calories a day. What is the more common amount of calories consumed by a male high school or college-level basketball player?

3. Eating what type of food immediately after a workout is recommended to refuel your body?

RESEARCH PROJECT:

Put together a balanced daily nutrition plan for yourself. Research how many calories you should be consuming given your age, height, and activity level. Be sure the plan includes the proper mix of fats, proteins, and carbohydrates.

IMAGERY

Imagery is a technique that has been embraced at the highest levels of several sports. It is the term used to describe the **enhancement** to the technique of visualization. It involves simulating competition by seeing it in your mind. Imagery takes visualization to the next level. Imagery is multisensory, so athletes are trained and encouraged to not only see their performance unfolding but to imagine the sounds and even the smells as well.

"The more an athlete can image the entire package, the better it's going to be," said United States Olympic team psychologist Nicole Detling. Detling, an assistant professor at the University of Utah, was one of nine sports psychologists to accompany the U.S. team to the Olympic Winter Games in Sochi in 2014. The Canadian team brought eight psychologists, and the Norwegians brought three.

Imagery is commonly used in basketball as well. In fact, basketball players tend to take it one step further. Players like two-time MVP Steve Nash used to take three or four imaginary free throw shots every time he stepped to the foul line before taking an actual shot.

Two-time NBA MVP Steve Nash used the technique of dynamic imagery throughout his career.

Nash was not only visualizing a successful shot, but he was also going through the correct physical motions to make the shot successful. This is known as dynamic imagery, which helps to stabilize the motor pattern that will be used for the action.

The key to imagery is to envision situations as

WORDS TO UNDERSTAND:

ascribed: to credit or assign, as to a cause or source

folded: failed or closed, especially in business

mantle: an important role or responsibility that passes from one person to another

Chapter 5

BASKETBALL: FROM SET SHOTS TO SLAM DUNKS AND SMALL BALL

NAISMITH TO THE NBA

James Naismith was born in Canada in 1861. He moved to Massachusetts for a job teaching at the Springfield YMCA in 1891. In the late autumn of that year, his boss tasked him to come up with an activity for his students, who were indoor bound due to the harsh winter weather that blanketed New England.

Naismith's solution was a game that used a soccer ball, and although it combined elements of other popular sports, it was unique. His game matched two teams of nine players against each other in a gymnasium with peach baskets at opposite ends, each nailed to the wall ten feet above the floor. The object was to throw the soccer ball into the opposing team's peach basket. This was done using a two-handed set shot, taken with both feet planted on the ground, a shot that persisted in the game into the 1950s. Passing the ball through the air was the only way to move the ball from player to player. To begin the game and after each made basket, the ball was tossed in the air between two players at the center of the gym. The ball had to be retrieved from the baskets with use of a ladder every time.

Naismith had thirteen rules for his original game, including forbidding body contact, which was punished similarly to hockey in that the offending player had to sit out without substitution until the next basket was made. Other rules gave the opposing team a point if their rivals committed three consecutive fouls and determined the length of games to be two fifteen-minute halves with a five-minute halftime rest period.

The game, which Naismith called "basket ball," was an immediate sensation. Articles appeared in newspapers about the game in 1892. By 1898, Naismith

Julius "Dr. J" Erving was one of the first stars of the new ABA.

had been hired at the University of Kansas as the nation's very first college basketball coach.

In 1906, the familiar metal hoops, nets, and backboards replaced the cumbersome peach baskets. In 1909, the Intercollegiate Athletic Association of the United States (later the National Collegiate Athletic Association or NCAA) took control of oversight of the game from the fifteen-school committee that had been running it since 1905. The first NCAA men's basketball tournament was played in 1939.

Professional basketball leagues had existed since 1898, although most had failed. That changed forever with the formation of the Basketball Association of America (BBA) in 1946. The BAA competed with the already existing National Basketball League (NBL), which had been operating since it was formed 1937. The leagues coexisted until 1949 when the BAA absorbed the NBL to become the National Basketball Association (NBA).

The NBA was not an immediate success, shrinking from eleven teams in 1950 to just eight in 1954. Early stars of the league included George Mikan of the Minneapolis Lakers, Bill Russell of the Boston Celtics, and Wilt Chamberlain of the Philadelphia Warriors. This star power helped to strengthen the NBA, and the league expanded to fourteen teams by 1968, the year Russell and the Celtics won their ninth championship in ten years.

In 1967, the rival American Basketball Association (ABA) arrived on the professional scene. The new league signed several young stars, most notably Julius "Dr. J" Erving in 1971. The NBA continued to grow, however, adding four more franchises by 1974. Despite some success, including popularizing the slam dunk and the three-point shot, the ABA could not compete. In 1976 the ABA **folded**, and the NBA absorbed four of its seven remaining teams.

The biggest turning point in the history of the NBA came in 1979, when rookies Larry Bird and Earvin "Magic" Johnson joined the league in Boston and Los Angeles, respectively. Two of the greatest players in basketball history, the pair began a rivalry that returned each of their franchises to glory and dominated

The fortunes of the NBA soared when Hall of Famers Larry Bird (left) and Magic Johnson (right) dominated the league in the 1980s.

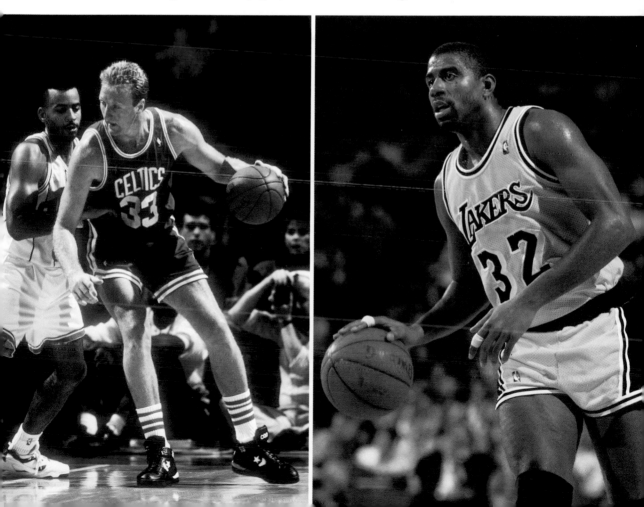

Legendary UCLA men's basketball coach John Wooden once led his Bruins teams to 88 consecutive victories, starting in 1971 and ending with a one point loss to Notre Dame in 1974. This is still the untouchable standard in men's basketball, but as far as NCAA Division I hoops go, this streak has been bested…twice.

On both occasions, the record breakers were the women's teams from the University of Connecticut. Coached by Geno Auriemma, the Huskies won 90 straight games between 2008 and 2010 before losing to Stanford. On January 14, 2017, the Huskies broke their own record with win number 91 in a row at SMU. Along the way, Auriemma's teams have won 11 national championships and counting, led by some of the best players in the history of women's basketball.

The best of these may have been shooting guard Diana Taurasi. Taurasi led the Huskies to three straight national championships from 2002, where the team went undefeated, to 2004. She was voted College Player of the Year in both her junior and senior years, and went on to be selected first overall in the 2004 WNBA draft.

The Women's NBA is a 12-team professional league that was started by the NBA in 1997. Half the teams are wholly owned and supported by NBA team owners. Taurasi was drafted by the Phoenix Mercury, one of only three original WNBA franchises that still play in its original market. Taurasi won three WNBA titles and was the 2009 WNBA MVP. She will retire as the all-time leading scorer in the history of the league.

Other great players in WNBA history include Tamika Catchings, Cynthia Cooper, Lisa Leslie, Lauren Jackson and Sheryl Swoopes.

the league for a decade. Johnson's Lakers won five of the next nine NBA titles, and Bird's Celtics won three. TV ratings spiked, and the league blossomed under its two superstars, paving the way for Michael Jordan.

Jordan was an NBA rookie in 1984 on a struggling Chicago Bulls team. After the 1991 season, Jordan took over the **mantle** as the NBA's premier player. He was already the only player to be named league MVP other than Bird and Johnson between 1984 and 1990, winning in 1988. In 1991, Jordan and the Bulls broke through with their first championship, beating the Lakers in Johnson's final season. He was also the NBA MVP that season. Jordan would go on to win five more championships and four more MVPs.

MARCH MADNESS AND KING JAMES

A decade before winning his first NBA title, Jordan won his first and only NCAA title by leading his University of North Carolina Tar Heels to victory in the men's basketball tournament. That was the year TV broadcaster CBS's commentator Brent Musburger referred to the NCAA tournament as "March Madness," co-opting the phrase used for the Illinois boy's state championship tournament coined by Henry Porter of the Illinois High School Association in 1939. Today, the NCAA tournament is a sixty-eight-team extravaganza and traditionally one of the most-watched sporting events (the title game moved from a broadcast to a cable network in 2016, which negatively affected viewership).

Despite the success of the men's basketball tournament, NCAA basketball lacks star power as the best players leave for the NBA after one college season.

The current college game lacks the stars who once headlined the tournament as the rules now allow the best players to leave for the NBA after one year in college. Before the NBA's so-called one-and-done rule was put in place in 2005, requiring players to be at least one year removed from high school to be eligible for the NBA entry draft, a kid from St. Vincent-St. Mary's high school in Akron, Ohio, entered the NBA straight out of high school, when he was drafted in June 2003, two months after Jordan retired. LeBron James was Jordan's heir apparent, and the 6'8" small forward has lived up to the billing.

James burst into the league and dominated like experts had predicted he would since he was a freshman at St. Vincent-St. Mary's, where he was dubbed "King James" and became the only three-time Mr. Basketball in the history of Ohio. James won the NBA Rookie of the Year award playing for his hometown Cleveland Cavaliers, averaging nearly twenty-one points and six assists a game. After leading the Cavaliers to the NBA Finals in 2007 and winning two MVP awards, James famously left Cleveland in 2010 to play with the Miami Heat.

James's departure from Cleveland was controversial to say the least. James's contract expired after the 2010 season, making him free to sign with any team. The Cavaliers offered him big money to stay. In a move that has been widely criticized, James made a spectacle of what is now known as "The Decision" by deciding to announce his choice during a nationally broadcast seventy-five-minute live television special exclusively about the announcement.

Watch a breakdown of NBA superstar LeBron James's famous pregame ritual.

LeBron James has dominated the NBA for the great part of this century.

Cavaliers owner Dan Gilbert wrote an open letter to fans that called The Decision a "cowardly betrayal," for which the NBA fined him $100,000. Some supported James's right to handle his free agency as he chose, but many others considered it dramatic self-promotion that disrespected the Cavaliers and all the teams that had made him an offer. In the end, however, it was a decision that ultimately paid off.

In Miami, James went to four consecutive NBA finals, helping the Heat win two of them. He opted to go back to Cleveland in 2015 and led his Cavaliers to back-to-back finals appearances and, in 2016, the first championship in franchise history. James competed in the NBA finals in successive years from 2011 to 2016.

Although James has been the primary force in the league in the twenty-first century, others have made an impact as well. Kevin Durant of Golden State is one of them. Durant, a 6'9" small forward, came into the league in 2007 after winning the Player of the Year award as a freshman at the University of Texas, his only year of college basketball. Durant was drafted by Seattle and won Rookie of the Year in his first season with the SuperSonics. The Sonics moved to Oklahoma City in 2008 and became the Thunder, and Durant continued to make it rain on the rest of the league. He averaged more than twenty-eight points per game in his eight seasons in Oklahoma City, leading the league in scoring four times. He led the Thunder to five straight playoff appearances, including a trip to the NBA finals in 2012, where the Thunder lost to James and the Heat. In 2014, Durant was named NBA MVP after averaging a career-high thirty-two points per game. Durant left Oklahoma City for Golden State in free agency in 2016.

Durant's Oklahoma City teammate Russell Westbrook is another of the game's best players. The 6'3" point guard is a threat to score a triple-double on any given night. Westbrook's athleticism separates him from any other player at his position and helps make him the best rebounding point guard in the NBA. Drafted by Seattle the year after Durant, Westbrook made the All-Rookie Team in his first season. In 2010 he hit his stride, beginning a string of seven straight seasons where he averaged more than twenty points per game. In 2015, Westbrook led the NBA in scoring at 28.1 points per game while also averaging more than seven rebounds and eight assists. In 2016, Westbrook signed a $28.5 million per year contract extension with Oklahoma City.

STEPHEN CURRY AND THE FUTURE OF BASKETBALL

As good as Durant, Westbrook, and even James have been, the best player in the NBA as of 2016 is Stephen Curry of Golden State. Curry was named league MVP in both 2015 and 2016, leading his team to the NBA finals in both seasons. Curry and the Warriors won the title over James and Cleveland in 2015 and blew a 3–1 lead in the 2016 to lose to James's team in 2016. Curry is considered by many to be the best pure shooter in the history of the sport, and his style of play is considered to be its future. Like James, Curry was born in Akron, but more than three years later, making Curry the younger player as James is into his thirties. Also like James, Curry's impact on the game is undeniable and may end up having the longest-lasting effect.

The success of Curry and the Warriors has made every coach and every team take notice. The Warriors not only won a championship, but they also won 140 games over the course of Curry's two MVP seasons,

Golden State's Stephen Curry takes a three-pointer from the corner in a game against Washington.

SIDEBAR
The Golden State Warriors Record-Breaking Season

The Golden State Warriors went 73–9 in 2015–2016, the best record in NBA history. Here are five eye-popping observations from the campaign:

1. Three-point shooting
For the second straight season, Stephen Curry broke the record for three-point field goals made, sinking 402. His previous record, set the season before, was 286. The only other player in history to make more than 275 threes in a season is Curry's backcourt partner, Klay Thompson, who hit 276 in 2015–2016. As a team, the Warriors also set the record for threes made with 1,077, 15 percent more than Houston made the previous season.

2. Losing streaks
Golden State lost nine games on the season. They followed up every one of those losses with a win. The Warriors had zero losing streaks, which had never been done before.

3. Winning streaks
It stands to reason that with seventy-three wins, there were many winning streaks on the season. The most remarkable of these was the first one. Golden State won its first twenty-four games, the best start to a season in NBA history.

4. Road Warriors
Golden State won a record thirty-four games on the road.

5. 50–45–90
Stephen Curry become only the third player to ever finish a regular season with shooting percentages above 50 percent from the field, 45 percent from beyond the arc, and 90 percent from the free-throw line. The only other players to do it are two-time MVP Steve Nash and Curry's coach with the Warriors, Steve Kerr, who won four titles with the Chicago Bulls in the 1990s.

including a league record seventy-three in 2015–2016. It is not only the fact that they have won more games than anyone else did but also the way they won them. The Warriors are not a big team. Curry is 6'3", and his backcourt partner Klay Thompson is 6'7". The other three regulars are 6'6" Andre Iguodala, 6'7" Draymond Green, and 6'8" Harrison Barnes. This relatively undersized lineup has been dubbed the "small ball" lineup, but its success has been huge.

All five Warriors can shoot, and they can handle the ball. Collectively, their shooting is just as effective from three-point range as it is from anywhere else, and they average more than 105 possessions per game, a staggeringly fast pace. Defensively, except for Curry, they can switch easily as they are all within a couple of inches in height. The small ball lineup outscored opponents by beating them at the three-point line. In 2015–2016, Curry set NBA records for three-point shots scored with 402. He took only 885, for

Draymond Green, seen here dunking the ball against Cleveland, is best known for his defensive skills.

a sizzling 45.4 percent. Thompson also shot better than 40 percent from behind the arc. In fact, all five regulars shot better than 35 percent from three-point range. Any one of the five could take and make a three at any time, making them almost impossible to defend.

A small lineup of ball handlers that can shoot from the perimeter is not the most revolutionary idea. What separates the Warriors, however, is the deadly accuracy of Curry and Thompson and the defensive prowess of Green, who led the team in rebounds and steals in 2015–2016. Coaches around the country at all levels have taken notice. The math is easy enough. Teams shoot about the same percentage on average from sixteen to twenty feet from the basket as they do from twenty-one feet, which would put them behind the arc and make the shot 50 percent more valuable when scored. It makes more sense to take more three-pointers instead of long, two-point jump shots. Coaches are beginning to warm to this strategy.

In 2015–2016, college coaches often attended Warrior practices, popping in to catch a glimpse behind the small ball curtain. Even more coaches had their NCAA Division I college teams watching Warriors game video. Eric Musselman, head coach of the University of Nevada's men's team, embraced small ball wholeheartedly that season, often playing five guards at once and using their quickness to create space and opportunities. He shows his team Warriors video four times a week. At the University of Southern California, Warriors video was part of the preseason program for the men's team. And at the University of Portland, coach Eric Reveno **ascribed** parts of his approach to watching the Warriors as well.

> Concentration and mental toughness are the margins of victory.
>
> – Bill Russell, Naismith Basketball Hall of Fame, 1975

"If you don't have shooters on the floor with all the scouting and stuff that's going on, the floor just gets very small because then (your opponent) doesn't have to guard certain shooters," Reveno said in an interview with USA Today early in 2016.

When he visited Warriors practice, Reveno took the opportunity to talk with Golden State coach Steve Kerr about his practice and instruction philosophy, with the intention of adapting the best parts of the Warriors philosophy to his own team's personnel. And personnel is the key. As much as small ball is catching on and may be the way of the future in the sport, it is one thing to try and play like Golden State, and quite another to be Golden State.

Davidson University's Bob McKillop coached Curry in college. "When Steph was with us, we actually had some very good shooters, but without Stephen Curry's presence, those shooters would have never gotten their shots," McKillop said in the USA Today interview. "And they got their shots because there was so much attention on Steph Curry."

Not many teams have a player that attracts the defense like Curry does, or can put five players on the court that shoot better than the league average from three-point range.

"I think with all of us, meaning college programs that might be playing somewhat like the Warriors, I think you can take bits and pieces, but I think to say that you can play like them, and use their philosophy, I think that's make-believe because everybody will try to be like them and just can't," Musselman told USA Today.

For two years, however, the model has been extremely successful, and nothing breeds imitation like success. As for recruiting the personnel to fit the philosophy, that is a big part of a college coach's job as well. The smallish dead-eye shooter may soon find himself in greater demand than the 6'10" forward. Small ball may change the game of basketball forever, or at least until the next successful system comes along.

TEXT-DEPENDENT QUESTIONS:

1. Who is known for creating the game of basketball?

2. Today, the NCAA tournament includes how many teams?

3. What is small ball?

RESEARCH PROJECT:

Look up the biggest stars of the early years of the NBA, before the 1976 NBA–ABA merger. Choose one player, and write a profile of him, briefly outlining his early years from discovering the game through high school, detailing his accomplishments at the collegiate level and the NBA, and indicating his impact on the league. Why was this player significant in NBA history?

SERIES GLOSSARY OF KEY TERMS

Acute Injury: Usually the result of a specific impact or traumatic event that occurs in one specific area of the body, such as a muscle, bone, or joint.

Calories: units of heat used to indicate the amount of energy that foods will produce in the human body.

Carbohydrates: substances found in certain foods (such as bread, rice, and potatoes) that provide the body with heat and energy and are made of carbon, hydrogen, and oxygen.

Cardiovascular: of or relating to the heart and blood vessels.

Concussion: a stunning, damaging, or shattering effect from a hard blow—especially a jarring injury of the brain resulting in a disturbance of cerebral function.

Confidence: faith in oneself and one's abilities without any suggestion of conceit or arrogance.

Cooldown: easy exercise, done after more intense activity, to allow the body to gradually transition to a resting or near-resting state.

Dietary Supplements: products taken orally that contain one or more ingredient (such as vitamins or amino acids) that are intended to supplement one's diet and are not considered food.

Dynamic: having active strength of body or mind.

Electrolytes: substances (such as sodium or calcium) that are ions in the body regulating the flow of nutrients into and waste products out of cells.

Flexible: applies to something that can be readily bent, twisted, or folded without any sign of injury.

Hamstrings: any of three muscles at the back of the thigh that function to flex and rotate the leg and extend the thigh.

Hydration: to supply with ample fluid or moisture.

Imagery: mental images, the products of imagination.

Mind-Set: a mental attitude or inclination.

Overuse Injury: an injury that is most likely to occur to the ankles, knees, hands, and wrists, due to the excessive use of these body parts during exercise and athletics.

Plyometrics: also known as "jump training" or "plyos," exercises in which muscles exert maximum force in short intervals of time, with the goal of increasing power (speed and strength).

Positive Mental Attitude (PMA): the philosophy that having an optimistic disposition in every situation in one's life attracts positive changes and increases achievement.

Protein: a nutrient found in food (as in meat, milk, eggs, and beans) that is made up of many amino acids joined together, is a necessary part of the diet, and is essential for normal cell structure and function.

Quadriceps: the greater extensor muscle of the front of the thigh that is divided into four parts.

Recovery: the act or process of becoming healthy after an illness or injury.

Resistance: relating to exercise, involving pushing against a source of resistance (such as a weight) to increase strength. Strength training, or resistance exercises, are those that build muscle. They create stronger and larger muscles by producing more and tougher muscle fibers to cope with the increasing weight demands.

Strategy: a careful plan or method.

Stretching: to extend one's body or limbs from a cramped, stooping, or relaxed position.

Tactics: actions or methods that are planned and used to achieve a particular goal.

Tendon: a tough piece of tissue in the body that connects a muscle to a bone.

Training: the process by which an athlete prepares for competition by exercising, practicing, and so on.

Warm-Up: exercise or practice especially before a game or contest—broadly, to get ready.

Workout: a practice or exercise to test or improve one's fitness for athletic competition, ability, or performance.

FURTHER READING:

Luke, Andrew. *Basketball (Inside the World of Sports)*. Broomall, PA: Mason Crest, 2017

Kelley, K.C. *Basketball Superstars 2015 (NBA Readers)*. New York: Scholastic Paperback Nonfiction, 2015.

Indovino, Shaina. *Lebron James (Superstars in the World of Basketball)*. Broomall, PA: Mason Crest, 2014

Gamble, Paul. *Strength and Conditioning for Team Sports: Sport-Specific Physical Preparation for High Performance*. Routledge: New York, NY, 2010

INTERNET RESOURCES:

Sports Injury Clinic: ***www.sportsinjuryclinic.net***

National Basketball Association: ***http://www.nba.com***

American Academy of Orthopedic Surgeons: ***http://www.aaos.org/ Education/SportsMedicine/***

Basketball Reference: ***http://www.basketball-reference.com/***

VIDEO CREDITS:

Check out Golden State superstar Steph Curry's warm-up routine: ***http://x-qr.net/1Gk8***

Check out this video of an X's and o's demo of an NBA play: ***http://x-qr. net/1HTm***

See NBA All-Star Chris Paul's workout video: ***http://x-qr.net/1GSB***

Watch NBA guard Ricky Rubio as he recovers from injury: ***http://x-qr. net/1HWk***

Watch a breakdown of NBA superstar LeBron James' famous pre-game ritual: ***http://x-qr.net/1His***

PICTURE CREDITS

QR CODES AND LINKS TO THIRD-PARTY CONTENT

INDEX

Abdul-Jabbar, Kareem, 16

acute injuries, 46

affirmations, 15

Allen, Ray, 26

American Basketball Association (ABA), 61

ankle and foot injuries, 47

Auriemma, Geno, 62

band-resisted backboard touches, 37

band-resisted layups, 37

Barnes, Harrison, 68

Basketball Association of America (BAA), 60

Bird, Larry, 61, *61*, 63

Boston Celtics, 26, 60, 61, 63

Butler, Caron, 24

Calderón, José, 13, *13*

carbohydrates, 8, 52, *53*

cardiovascular training, 39–42, *39*, *40*

cartilage injuries, 47–48

Catchings, Tamika, 62

Chamberlain, Wilt, 60

Chicago Bulls, *25*, 63, 67

Cleveland Cavaliers, 64–65, *65*, 66, *68*

college basketball, 62, 63, *63*, 69

conditioning tips, 31

cool-downs, 31

Cooper, Cynthia, 62

court conditions, 45–46

crunches, 36–37

Curry, Stephen
  about, 66–67, *66*, 68, 69, 70
  warm-up routines, 12, *12*

"The Decision," 64–65

Detling, Nicole, 22, 23

diet
  See nutrition

drills, 12

Durant, Kevin, 65

equipment, 45

Erving, Julius, *60*, 61

fast breaks, 20

fats, 54, *54*

finger injuries
  See hand, wrist, and finger injuries

flexibility exercises, 32–34, *33*

foot injuries
  See ankle and foot injuries

full-court press, 21

"game face," 7–8

"getting in the zone," 16

Gilbert, Dan, 65

In this index, page numbers in ***bold italics*** font indicate photos or videos.

give-and-go, 20

Golden State Warriors, *12*, 65, 66–70, *66*, *68*

Green, Draymond, 68, *68*

groin stretches, 34

hand, wrist, and finger injuries, 49

head injuries, 51–52

Hill, George, 12

history, 59–60

Hornacek, Jeff, 24

Hull, Lamar, 10

Iguodala, Andre, 68

imagery and visualization, 15, 22–23

injury incidence, 45

injury prevention, 11, 29, 46

injury rehabilitation, *48*

injury types, 46–52

Intercollegiate Athletic Association of the United States, 60

Jackson, Lauren, 62

James, LeBron
about, 64–65, *65*
pregame rituals, 64
quote, 9
superstitions, 24, 26

Johnson, Earvin "Magic," 61, *61*, 63

Jordan, Michael
about, *14*, *25*, 63
quotes, 14, 15
superstitions, 26

Karl, George, 11

Kerr, Steve, 67, 69

Knight, Bob, 19

Korver, Kyle, 11

late game fouls, 21

leg injuries, 48–49

Leslie, Lisa, 62

Los Angeles Lakers, *61*, 63

lying crossovers, 34

"March Madness," 63

McKillop, Bob, 70

meditation, 23

mental routines, 14–16, 22–23

Miami Heat, 65

Mikan, George, 60

Milwaukee Bucks, *29*

Musberger, Brent, 63

Muscala, Mike, 8

Musselman, Eric, 69, 70

Naismith, James, 59–60

Nash, Steve, 8, 22–23, *22*, 67

National Basketball Association (NBA), 60

National Basketball League (NBL), 60

National Collegiate Athletic Association (NCAA), 60

  See also "March Madness"

neck injuries, 51

nutrition, 8, 52–54

off-season fitness, 32, 39, *39*

Oklahoma City Thunder, 65, 66

O'Neal, Shaquille, 24

overuse injuries, 46

Paul, Chris, *32*

Philadelphia 76ers, *29*, *60*

pick and roll, 20

planks, 36

plank ski jumps, 38–39

playbooks

  See strategies

plyometric exercises, 38–39, *38*

pointed toes, 33

Porter, Henry, 63

proteins, 53–54, 53

protein supplements, 55–56

relaxed attention, 23

resistance training, 36–37, *36*, *37*

Reveno, Eric, 69

R.I.C.E. treatment, 46, 50

rituals and routines, *64*

  See also superstitions

Rondo, Rajan, 24

rope jumping, 11, *38*

Rubio, Ricky, 48

rule changes, 63–64

Russell, Bill, 7, *9*, 60

shootarounds, 13–14

shoulder injuries, 49–51

side lunges, 33

skier, 38

sleep, 9–10

speed dribble with harness, 37

sports psychologists, 15–16

strategies, *19*, 20–21, *20*, *21*

stretching, 10–11, *30*

Summitt, Pat, 10

superstitions, 24, 26

supplements, 54–56, *55*, *56*

Swoopes, Sheryl, 62

Taurasi, Diana, 62

Terry, Jason, 26

Thomas, Isiah, 16

Thompson, Klay, 67, 68, 69

time-outs, 21

University of Connecticut Huskies, 62

U.S. Consumer Product Safety Commission, 45

visualization
  See imagery and visualization
vitamins, 55
warm-up routines, 11–12, 29–31, *32*
  See also flexibility exercises
weight training, *35*
  See also resistance training
Westbrook, Russell, 65–66
Women's NBA (WNBA), 62
Wooden, John, 7, 7, 62
wrist injuries
  See hand, wrist, and finger injuries

ABOUT THE AUTHOR

Peter Douglas is a former journalist, reporting on both sports and general news for many years at television stations in various locations across the US affiliated with NBC, CBS and Fox. Prior to his journalism career he worked with the Boston Red Sox Major League baseball team. An avid writer and sports enthusiast, he has authored 16 additional books on sports topics. In his downtime Peter enjoys family time with his wife and two young children and attending hockey and baseball games in his home city.